WHAT WE GET FROM EGYPTIAN MYTHOLOGY

LISA OWINGS

Published in the United States of America
by Cherry Lake Publishing
Ann Arbor, Michigan
www.cherrylakepublishing.com

Consultants: Noreen Doyle, Research Associate, University of Arizona Egyptian Expedition; Marla Conn, ReadAbility, Inc.
Editorial direction and book production: Red Line Editorial

Photo Credits: Philip Bird/Shutterstock Images, cover, 1; Nemar74/Shutterstock Images, 5; Roger Wood/Corbis, 7; Don Mammoser/Shutterstock Images, 9; Werner Forman/Werner Forman Archive/Corbis, 11; Dorling Kindersley/ Thinkstock, 13, 17; Sandro Vannini/Corbis, 15; bopra77/Shutterstock Images, 18; Brian S./Shutterstock Images, 21; Orhan Cam/Shutterstock Images, 23 (left); meunierd/Shutterstock Images, 23 (right); mountainpix/Shutterstock Images, 25; Universal Pictures/Everett Collection, 27; The Washington Post/Getty Images, 28

Library of Congress Cataloging-in-Publication Data

Owings, Lisa, author.
  What we get from Egyptian mythology / by Lisa Owings.
    pages cm. -- (Mythology and culture)
  Includes index.
  ISBN 978-1-63188-912-7 (hardcover : alk. paper) -- ISBN 978-1-63188-928-8 (pbk. : alk. paper) -- ISBN 978-1-63188-944-8 (pdf) -- ISBN 978-1-63188-960-8 (hosted ebook)
  1. Mythology, Egyptian--Juvenile literature. 2. Civilization--Egyptian influences--Juvenile literature. 3. Egypt--Civilization--Juvenile literature. I. Title.

  BL2441.3.O95 2015
  398.2'0932--dc23

                    2014029989

Cherry Lake Publishing would like to acknowledge the work of
The Partnership for 21st Century Skills. Please visit www.p21.org
for more information.

Printed in the United States of America
Corporate Graphics
December 2014

ABOUT THE AUTHOR

Lisa Owings has a degree in English and creative writing from the University of Minnesota. She has written and edited a wide variety of educational books for young people. Owings lives in Andover, Minnesota, with her husband and a small menagerie of pets.

TABLE OF CONTENTS

CHAPTER 1

LIFE IN ANCIENT EGYPT

Life in ancient Egypt revolved around the Nile River and the sun. People first made their homes in Egypt around 3000 BCE. They farmed in the fertile Nile valley, a ribbon of green against the scorching desert. Every year, the Nile flooded the land. These floods brought rich soils for planting and attracted wildlife for hunting. Every day, the sun rose to nourish the land and its people.

Egyptians raised cattle to help with the hard, important work of farming. Cattle also provided milk

For thousands of years, the Nile River has made it possible for people to live in Egypt's desert.

and meat. People used local materials to build boats for fishing and traveling along the river. Over time, Egyptians organized life and work in small towns. Eventually they built great cities.

Ancient Egyptians believed their lives were blessed. They saw that their environment provided them with plentiful food, material goods, and warmth. The Nile River was used for transport and to water crops. At the same time, they knew the desert sun could be deadly, and Nile floods could bring destruction. These opposing forces shaped the earliest Egyptian **myths**.

Myths are stories people tell to explain how the world works and how it was created. These stories usually take place in ancient times. They often tell how gods and goddesses shaped the universe.

Sun gods are the most important figures in Egyptian myths. The waters of the Nile also influenced Egyptian myths. In creation myths, life was often brought forth from the water. Gods of the sky and **underworld** traveled by boat, just as Egyptians did on the Nile. Egyptian gods often took the forms of familiar animals of the Nile valley. Cattle gods were common. Other Egyptian gods looked like **jackals**, cats, birds, snakes, and scarab beetles. These associations came from everyday experiences with these animals. Jackals were

LOOK AGAIN

LOOK AT THIS IMAGE CLOSELY. WHAT CAN YOU LEARN FROM IT ABOUT EVERYDAY LIFE IN ANCIENT EGYPT?

seen digging around in cemeteries. This behavior inspired the creation of Anubis, a jackal-headed god of death.

The principle of *ma'at*—order, truth, and balance—ruled Egyptian society. Egyptians believed they lived in a bubble of orderly creation. Outside this bubble was **chaos**, always threatening to destroy their world.

Egyptian societies centered on the **pharaoh**, a title used for an ancient Egyptian ruler. It was the pharaoh's job to maintain *ma'at* and keep away chaos. Egyptian myths held that pharaohs were children of gods and partly **divine**. These stories protected the pharaoh's power. Any act against the pharaoh was an act against the gods and *ma'at*.

Religion was part of daily life for all Egyptians. Art, language, **rituals**, and everyday objects were all connected to worship of the gods. Ancient Egyptians also believed in eternal life after death. If they could live by *ma'at* and arrange for a proper burial, the gods would welcome them into a pleasant **afterlife**.

For most Egyptians, the afterlife would be similar to life on Earth. They were buried with food, drink, and other supplies to use in the afterlife. They also needed instructions on making the dangerous journey through the underworld. Myths about this journey were painted on tombs, coffins, or scrolls to guide the dead.

The elaborate pyramid tombs of the pharaohs show how important the afterlife was to ancient Egyptians.

CHAPTER 2

MANY GODS

Egyptian myths are full of gods that have shifting stories and identities. At first, each ancient Egyptian town worshiped its own gods. Each town created its own myths. Then the people began to gather in larger cities. Beliefs changed depending on the location or the pharaoh who was in charge.

One key type of belief is the creation myth. These myths explain how the world came to be. In one widely known Egyptian creation myth, in the beginning, everything was watery chaos. The dark waters were

Isis was first worshipped more than 4,000 years ago.

called Nun. They were believed to be the source of the
Nile. From these waters, the young sun god Atum
emerged as the first sunrise.

Soon Atum grew lonely. From his mouth he spit the
first pair of beings, Shu and Tefnut. Shu was the god of
air, and Tefnut was the goddess of moisture. Tefnut gave
birth to Geb, the earth god, and Nut, the sky goddess.

Geb and Nut had four children. They were Osiris,
Seth, Isis, and Nephthys. Isis, a goddess of mothers,

became the wife of Osiris, a god of order. Nephthys, a goddess of death, was the wife of Seth, a god of chaos. Humans were later created from Atum's tears of joy.

In the creation myth of the Egyptian city of Memphis, the creator god made the world with his heart and tongue. His heart desired things to be created. Then he spoke their names, and they came into being.

After the creator god had ruled for a while, he left Earth to live in the heavens. Osiris was chosen to rule in his place. Osiris and Isis became king and queen of all Egypt. They ruled well and justly. But their brother, Seth, became jealous. He wanted the throne for himself. So he murdered Osiris. He locked his brother in a chest and threw him in the river.

Isis soon learned of her husband's death. She searched far and wide and finally found the chest. Before she could bury Osiris, Seth stole the body. He scattered pieces of it throughout the country. Isis found all the pieces and put Osiris's body back together.

Horus is depicted with a bird's head.

She was able to bring her husband back to life just long enough for her to bear their son. Osiris was later **mummified** and given eternal life as a ruler and judge of the underworld. He had the power to give others life after death.

In the myth, Isis gave birth to her son, Horus, in secret. When Horus grew up, he fought Seth for the throne. In the most popular versions of this myth, Horus won the right to rule all of Egypt.

For ancient Egyptians, each sunrise represented renewal. Egyptian myths held that the sun god Ra was born anew each morning. He traveled across the sky in a boat each day. Then the sky goddess Nut swallowed him for the night. She would give birth to him again the next morning.

Later myths told of Ra's journey through the underworld each night. With the help of others, he had to defeat the monsters of the underworld. Ra's greatest enemy was the demon snake Apophis. The sun god battled the snake every night and always won. Before each dawn, the battle-weary Ra became one with Osiris, a symbol of both death and life. Then the sun god was reborn and started his journey anew.

LOOK AGAIN

CHAPTER 3

Egyptian Myths in Other Cultures

Egyptians traded goods and stories with nearby peoples. Some of these cultures were influenced by Egyptian religion and **mythology**. Jewish, Christian, Greek, and Roman myths all show some similarities to Egyptian stories.

Starting in the 600s BCE, war forced many Jews to leave what is now Israel. Some Jewish people sought refuge in Egypt. They learned about Egyptian gods and their stories. Experts believe Egyptian myths influenced the Hebrew Bible, which was still being written at the time. This sacred text became the Old Testament of the Christian Bible.

The creation stories of Judaism and Christianity begin with one god creating the world. They are similar to the Memphis creation myth, in which the creator god uses speech. In Judaism and Christianity, God creates the world in the same way. He says, "Let there be . . ."

Ancient Egyptians shared their religious ideas within their communities and with the outsiders they encountered.

The Greeks and Romans built temples dedicated to the worship of Isis.

and speaks what he wishes to create. Whatever he speaks comes to be.

Egypt came under the rule of the Greeks during the 300s BCE. Greek rulers served as pharaohs. The Greeks saw many similarities between Egyptian and Greek gods. They identified Horus with the youthful Greek sun god Apollo. The Egyptian sun god Amun was similar to Zeus, king of the Greek gods. Osiris was compared with the Greek god of wine and fertility, Dionysus.

Isis and Osiris became some of the most important gods to the Greeks. Isis in particular was worshipped as the ideal woman and mother. She had been powerful enough to bring Osiris back to life. Cleopatra, a Greek pharaoh of Egypt, compared herself to Isis. The Greek author Plutarch also wrote one of the most popular versions of the Isis-Osiris myth.

Roman rulers later took control of Egypt in 30 BCE. The Romans also came to worship Isis and Osiris. They were drawn to the promise of eternal life. The worship of Isis and Osiris spread throughout the Mediterranean region.

GO DEEPER

REREAD THIS CHAPTER CLOSELY. WHAT IS ITS MAIN IDEA? FIND THREE PIECES OF EVIDENCE TO SUPPORT YOUR POINT.

CHAPTER 4

PYRAMIDS AND HIEROGLYPHS

The pyramid is the most famous symbol of Egypt. The Pyramids of Giza were built as tombs for pharaohs more than 4,500 years ago. These giant structures were meant to help the pharaohs enter the afterlife. The walls of some pyramids were covered in images and an ancient form of writing called **hieroglyphs**. The images and writing inside tombs are some of the richest sources of Egyptian art and myths.

The great pyramids of Egypt have inspired other countries to build similar structures. One famous

The Luxor, a hotel and casino in Las Vegas, Nevada, is modeled after Egyptian pyramids.

pyramid is the large glass pyramid at the entrance to the art museum known as the Louvre, located in Paris, France. The pyramid was built in 1989. The architect, I. M. Pei, based his design on the Pyramids of Giza. Three smaller glass pyramids surround the main one. Another example of the influence of pyramids is the pyramid on the back of the U.S. dollar bill. It was chosen as a symbol of enduring strength.

Pyramids are not the only parts of Egyptian religious culture to inspire later people. Throughout the 1800s, architecture in Europe and North America was inspired by Egyptian tombs and temples.

Tall, pointed **obelisks** covered in Egyptian hieroglyphs were popular structures. Two obelisks from an Egyptian temple were removed in the 1800s. One was shipped to Britain. It still stands on the banks of the river Thames in London. The other was given to the United States and placed in New York City's Central Park. The Washington Monument was inspired by Egyptian obelisks. It was built in Washington, DC, in 1884 to honor the first U.S. president, George Washington. The monument was the world's tallest structure when it was built. It stands 555 feet (169 m) tall.

To the Egyptians, hieroglyphs were said to be the words of the gods. The symbols were thought to have sacred power. Care was taken not to write about bad or dangerous things in hieroglyphs in case those things became real.

In 1922, British **archaeologist** Howard Carter discovered the tomb of King Tutankhamen, commonly

LOOK AGAIN

Examine the Washington Monument, left, and an ancient Egyptian obelisk, right. What similarities and differences do you see?

known as King Tut. A golden mask and other treasures were hidden inside. These finds inspired another wave of interest in everything Egyptian. The Art Deco style of art and architecture drew on Egyptian themes during the 1920s. Artists used images of shining suns and other religious symbols of Egypt.

Egyptian images and symbols found in tombs, such as King Tut's, remain popular today. The ankh is a cross with a loop at the top. It represents life, especially after death. The ankh symbol is often used in jewelry. The wedjat eye, or Eye of Horus, is another common symbol. In the Osiris myth, Seth rips out Horus's eye during battle. Another god heals his eye. This myth made the Eye of Horus a powerful symbol of healing and protection. Many Egyptians, including King Tut, wore jewelry with this symbol. People from diverse cultures today continue the tradition.

The golden mask of King Tut captured the public's
imagination when it was discovered.

CHAPTER 5

THE MODERN MYTHOLOGY

The richness of ancient Egyptian mythology makes it a popular subject for movies, television shows, and modern stories. Mummies, one of the most famous parts of Egyptian culture, are closely linked to mythology. They have become popular subjects for movies and books.

The 1999 adventure film *The Mummy* explores the idea of a mummy coming back to life. In the film, a pharaoh's priest is cursed, mummified, and buried alive.

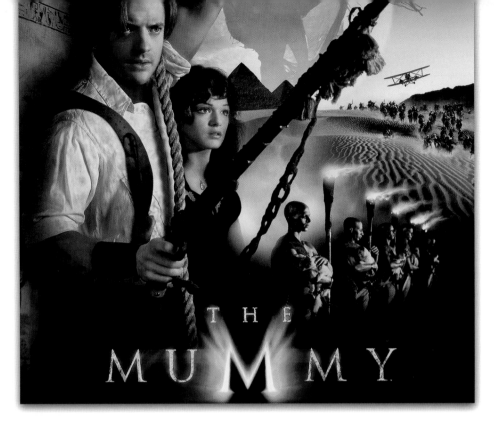

The Mummy *does not feature accurate Egyptian mythology, but it shows the public is still interested in ancient Egypt.*

Thousands of years later, a group of explorers finds the priest's tomb. They accidentally bring his mummy back to life. The priest unleashes his curse on the land. The explorers are left struggling to defeat him.

In *The Mummy*, ancient Egyptians have the power to bring people back to life, and mummification seems like a form of punishment. But in ancient Egypt, mummification was an important part of people's

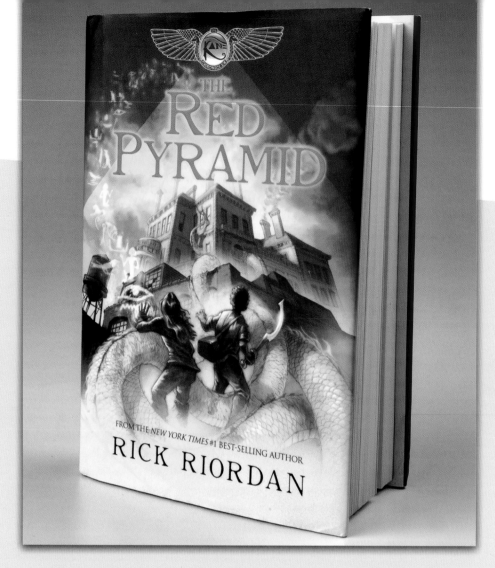

The Red Pyramid *is the first book in the Kane Chronicles series.*

religious views. In their mythology, mummification made sure the deceased would enjoy an afterlife.

Rick Riordan's Kane Chronicles series of books also features Egyptian mythology. In the series, Egyptian gods are accidentally and magically transported to the modern world. Two children, Carter and Sadie, try to cast them out of the real world.

Egyptian mythology has also appeared in video games. The game *Smite* lets players choose to play as one of many different Egyptian gods, including Geb, Isis, and Osiris. Huge battles unfold that also involve gods from the Roman, Greek, and Norse mythologies.

The world still has much to learn about Egyptian myths and culture. Archaeologists continue to make new discoveries about how the Egyptians lived and what they believed. It is fascinating to discover how these myths have survived thousands of years to enrich cultures all around the world today.

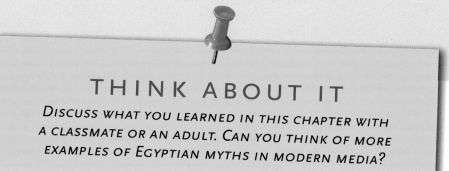

THINK ABOUT IT

DISCUSS WHAT YOU LEARNED IN THIS CHAPTER WITH A CLASSMATE OR AN ADULT. CAN YOU THINK OF MORE EXAMPLES OF EGYPTIAN MYTHS IN MODERN MEDIA?

THINK ABOUT IT

- In Chapters One and Two, you learned how Egypt's landscape influenced its mythology. How might the gods or myths have been different if the ancient Egyptians had lived near you?

- In Chapter Two, you learned about Egyptian creation stories. What is a creation story from your culture? Do you notice similarities to Egyptian creation stories? What are those similarities?

- What were you most surprised to find has come from Egyptian mythology? Can you think of something else in your everyday life that may have been inspired by ancient Egypt?

LEARN MORE

FURTHER READING

Boyer, Crispin. *National Geographic Kids: Everything Ancient Egypt*. Washington, DC: National Geographic, 2011.

Napoli, Donna Jo. *Treasury of Egyptian Mythology: Classic Stores of Gods, Goddesses, Monsters & Mortals*. Washington, DC: National Geographic, 2013.

Putman, James. *Pyramid*. New York: DK Publishing, 2011.

WEB SITES

Egyptian Gods
http://www.landofpyramids.org
This Web site features more information about several ancient Egyptian gods.

Ten Facts about Ancient Egypt
http://www.ngkids.co.uk/did-you-know/ten-facts-about-ancient-egypt
Check out this Web site for 10 interesting facts about Egypt and ancient Egyptians.

GLOSSARY

afterlife (AF-tur-life) life after death

archaeologist (ark-kee-OL-uh-jist) a person who studies ancient peoples through the objects those people have left behind

chaos (KAY-oss) a state of complete disorder

divine (duh-VINE) godlike or coming from the gods

hieroglyphs (HYE-ruh-glifs) ancient Egyptian writing

jackals (JAK-uhlz) wild dogs that live in Africa and Asia

mummified (MUH-mi-fyd) preserved by treating with oils and wrapping in strips of cloth

mythology (mi-THOL-uh-jee) a collection of myths dealing with a culture's gods or heroes

myths (MITHS) stories that attempt to describe the origin of a people's customs or beliefs or to explain mysterious events

obelisks (AH-beh-lisks) stone pillars often used as monuments

pharaoh (FAIR-oh) a title for an ancient Egyptian ruler

rituals (RICH-oo-uhlz) formal acts that are always done in the same way

underworld (UHN-dur-wurld) a land of the dead

INDEX